# MULAN

## LEVEL 6

Re-told by: Paul Shipton
Series Editor: Melanie Williams

**Pearson Education Limited**
Edinburgh Gate, Harlow,
Essex CM20 2JE, England
and Associated Companies throughout the world.

ISBN: 978-1-4082-8875-7

This edition first published by Pearson Education Ltd 2012

9 10 8

Set in 15/19pt OT Fiendstar
Printed in China
SWTC/08

Published by Pearson Education Ltd.

For a complete list of the titles available in the Pearson English Kids Readers series, please go to
www.pearsonenglishkidsreaders.com. Alternatively, write to your local Pearson Education office or to
Pearson English Readers Marketing Department, Pearson Education, Edinburgh Gate, Harlow, Essex CM202JE, England.

Centuries ago in China, there was a young woman. Her name was Mulan, and she lived with her parents and grandmother.

Mulan loved her family and she wanted to bring honor to them. But at that time there was only one way for a young woman to do that – she had to marry a good husband.

"A wife must be quiet, polite, and pleasant at all times," Mulan said sadly to herself. "But that isn't *me*! I can never be a perfect wife or a perfect daughter."

Mulan's father Fa Zhou joined her in the garden. He did not like his daughter to be unhappy. He did not want her to worry about the future.

"Look at the flowers," Fa Zhou said to her. He waved an arm at the pink flowers all around them. Then he pointed to one little flower. "That one has not opened yet … but it will be the loveliest flower of all."

Mulan smiled. Her father was talking about her.

Suddenly, there was a noise from the village – the sound of horses.

"What's happening?" asked Mulan.

Someone came to the village with bad news. His name was Chi Fu and he worked for the Emperor of China.

"The Huns have attacked China," Chi Fu said. "The Emperor has ordered one man from every family to fight in his army."

When Chi Fu began to read the names of different families, Mulan watched from behind a wall.

At last Chi Fu said the words that Mulan was afraid to hear, "the Fa family."

Mulan's father was the only man in the Fa family. He went to receive his orders.

"I am ready to fight," he said.

Mulan could not listen any longer.

She ran out and cried, "No! Father, you can't go!" She looked up at Chi Fu on his horse. "My father fought bravely in the Emperor's army years ago. He can't fight now — he is *sick*."

"Be quiet!" shouted Chi Fu angrily. He turned to Mulan's father. "You must teach your daughter to be silent!" he said.

Fa Zhou said quietly, "Mulan, you do not bring honor on our family."

He took his orders and walked back to his house without another word.

"Be at the army camp tomorrow!" Chi Fu shouted after him.

At dinner that night the family ate silently and listened to the storm outside.

At last, Mulan said, "Father, you *can't* go and fight in the army!"

Fa Zhou spoke slowly. "It is an honor to fight for my country and my family."

"So you will die for honor?" Mulan asked.

"I will do *what is right*!" said Fa Zhou angrily.

Mulan turned and ran from the house. She sat under the Great Stone Dragon outside and cried in the rain. Her father was too old and too sick to fight, but he was too proud to tell anyone.

How could Mulan stop Fa Zhou?

Suddenly, she had an idea. She ran quickly to the room where her father kept his sword and armor. She took down the sharp sword and cut off her long, dark hair. Then she put on her father's armor.

With her short hair and her father's armor, Mulan looked just like a young soldier. *She* could join the army and her father could stay at home.

She put Fa Zhou's orders in her pocket and went outside to wake her horse.

Mulan looked at her family home for the last time and then she rode into the night.

It was still dark when Mulan's grandmother woke up.

"Mulan!" she cried. "Mulan has gone!"

Mulan's parents jumped up. They could not find their daughter anywhere.

Fa Zhou ran to the armor room. His sword and armor were not there. When he saw this, Fa Zhou understood. "She has gone to join the army," he said.

"You must go after her," Mulan's mother cried. "She might die."

"If I go after her, she *will* die," said Fa Zhou. "The army will kill her."

Mulan's grandmother closed her eyes. "Ancestors, please hear me," she said quietly. "Keep Mulan safe."

The wind carried her words into the temple where the Fa family's ancestors lay. The First Ancestor heard Mulan's grandmother.

"Mushu, wake up," he said.

A strange light shone in the temple, and suddenly a little stone dragon was alive. His name was Mushu.

"I'm *ready!*" he cried. "*I'll* keep the Fa family safe!"

"That isn't your job," said the First Ancestor. "Your job is to wake up the other ancestors."

"Okay," said Mushu unhappily. "I'll wake them up."

Soon all the ancestors were awake.

"We must send someone to keep Mulan safe," said one ancestor.

"Okay, I'll go!" cried Mushu.

The ancestors laughed. "We must send a *real* dragon, not YOU!" said the First Ancestor. "Go and wake up the Great Stone Dragon."

Mushu went into the garden where the stone dragon sat.

"Wake up!" Mushu shouted. But the big stone dragon did not wake up. It did not become alive. It just fell into a thousand little pieces.

"What am I going to do now?" asked Mushu. Then he had an idea. "*I'll* do the job. *I'll* go and keep Mulan safe!"

Far from home, Mulan was practicing "being a man" before she went into the army camp.

"Remember," she told herself. "Men and women don't talk and act in the same way."

Suddenly, a dark shape moved behind the fire.

"I AM HERE TO HELP YOU!" cried a loud voice.

"Who are you?" asked Mulan nervously.

"I am the greatest ... the strongest ..." He walked out from behind a rock. "I am MUSHU!"

Mulan looked down at this strange little animal. "What *are* you?"

"A dragon!" cried Mushu. "Your ancestors sent me to help you!"

When Mulan walked into the camp, Mushu hid inside her jacket.

"Remember – you must be a man now," the little dragon said.

Mulan looked carefully at one of the other new soldiers.

"What are you looking at?" said the man.

"Hit him," Mushu said quietly. "That's how men say hello."

So Mulan hit the soldier. He tried to hit back, but he missed Mulan. He hit a different soldier.

That was just the start. Soon a lot of the soldiers were fighting until ...

"Stop!" shouted a deep voice.

It was Captain Shang.

"Who started this trouble?" Shang asked. All of the new soldiers pointed at Mulan.

"Er, I'm sorry," said Mulan in her deepest "man" voice.

"What's your name, soldier?" asked Shang.

Mulan thought quickly – she could not give her real name. "I'm ... Ping!"

Shang turned to the other soldiers. "You must all clean this camp from top to bottom. You can thank your new friend Ping for this job," he said.

The other soldiers looked angrily at Mulan.

"Tomorrow you will begin the hard work," Shang continued. "You're going to become *real* soldiers!"

Early the next morning, the new soldiers stood before Shang. He shot an arrow into the top of a tall pole.

He pointed at one soldier and said, "Yao, get that arrow."

Yao went to the bottom of the pole, but Shang shouted, "Wait! You must carry these with you." He gave two heavy, round weights to Yao.

It was impossible for Yao to climb the pole. Another soldier tried, then another. No one could climb and get the arrow.

"When one of you reaches the arrow, you will all be ready to fight in the army," Shang said.

"A good soldier must be a real man," Shang explained. "He must be strong and fast. He must be brave." He looked at all of the new soldiers around him. "We've got a lot of work to do."

Shang taught the soldiers to fight with long sticks and with their hands. He taught them to shoot arrows and use the army's cannons.

At first Mulan and the others could not do anything.

Mulan was not as strong as some of the others, but she worked hard. Slowly all the new soldiers became better and better. They were becoming *real* soldiers.

One night Mulan looked up at the arrow at the top of the pole. She had an idea.

With the two heavy weights around her wrists, she began to climb. She used the weights to stop herself from falling back down. It was slow, difficult work. Mulan's arms hurt, her legs hurt, but she refused to stop.

When the other soldiers came out of their tents in the morning, she was still climbing.

"Look at Ping!" somebody shouted.

At last, Mulan reached the top and threw the arrow to the ground. The soldiers were ready!

Before they left the camp, Mulan decided to swim in the lake.

She was in the water when suddenly three of the other soldiers — Yao, Chien-Po, and Ling — jumped into the water, too. They wanted to be friends with "Ping" now.

Mulan was nervous the soldiers might find out her secret.

Mushu saw them too, and swam toward them.

"A snake!" cried Ling when he saw the little red dragon.

The three men began to shout and hit the water. Quickly Mulan got out of the water and into her clothes. She was Ping again.

Far from the camp, Shan-Yu and his army of Huns were near the mountains.

Shan-Yu pointed. "The quickest way to the Emperor is through those mountains," he said. "But the Chinese army is waiting for us at a village there."

"We can take a *different* path," said one of his men. "We can go *around* the mountains."

Shan-Yu smiled. "I don't *want* to take a different path. We're going to go into those mountains and we're going to give the Chinese army a surprise. And then nothing can stop us. The Emperor's city is ours."

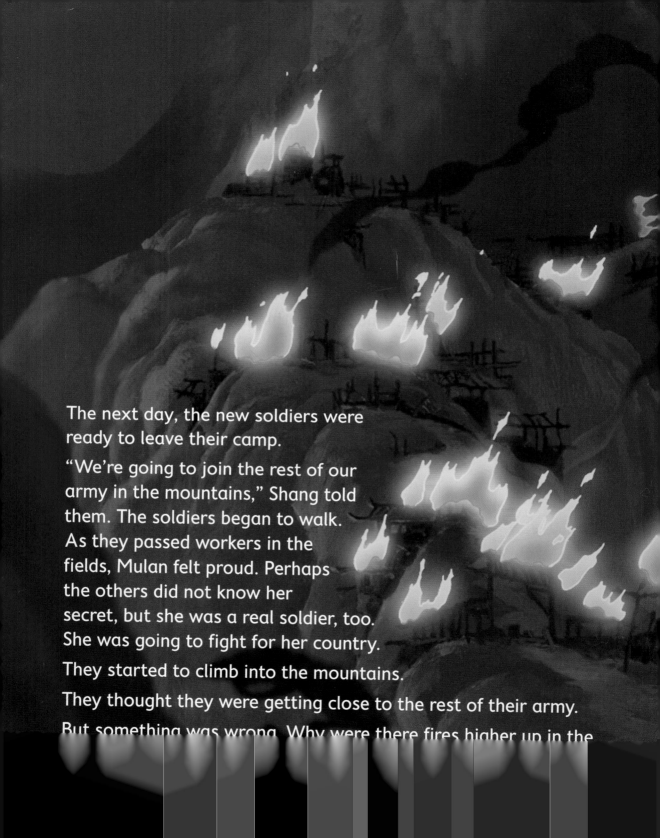

The next day, the new soldiers were ready to leave their camp.

"We're going to join the rest of our army in the mountains," Shang told them. The soldiers began to walk. As they passed workers in the fields, Mulan felt proud. Perhaps the others did not know her secret, but she was a real soldier, too. She was going to fight for her country.

They started to climb into the mountains.

They thought they were getting close to the rest of their army.

But something was wrong. Why were there fires higher up in the

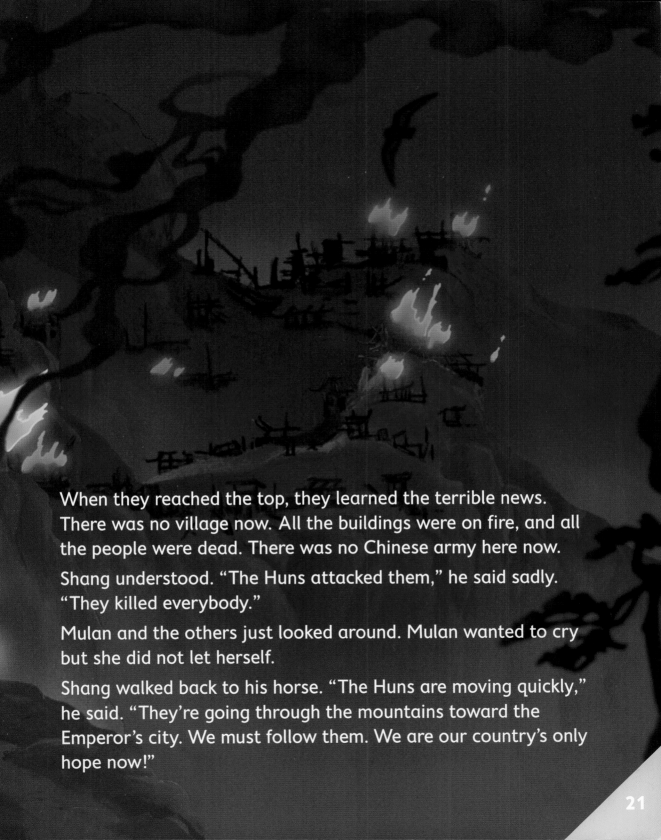

When they reached the top, they learned the terrible news. There was no village now. All the buildings were on fire, and all the people were dead. There was no Chinese army here now.

Shang understood. "The Huns attacked them," he said sadly. "They killed everybody."

Mulan and the others just looked around. Mulan wanted to cry but she did not let herself.

Shang walked back to his horse. "The Huns are moving quickly," he said. "They're going through the mountains toward the Emperor's city. We must follow them. We are our country's only hope now!"

The snow was deeper high in the mountains. It became harder to walk, but the soldiers did not stop.

Suddenly, there was a sound and hundreds of arrows were flying toward them. The Huns were attacking!

"Move!" Shang shouted to his men.

They shot one of the cannons higher up the mountain. When the cannon smoke disappeared, they could see the enemy. There were *hundreds* of them, high on the hill, all on horses. Shan-Yu shouted something and the Huns began to attack.

"Prepare to fight," Shang told his men. "If we die, we will die with honor."

Shan-Yu was at the front of his men.

"Shoot the cannon at *him*!" shouted Shang.

But Mulan had another idea. She took the cannon. She put it into the snow, then looked up quickly. Shan-Yu was racing toward her. His sword was in his hand and his horse was running fast through the snow.

"Quick!" shouted Mushu from inside Mulan's jacket. Mulan shot the cannon.

"You missed!" cried Mushu. But Mulan was not trying to hit Shan-Yu. She wanted to hit the top of a mountain high above the enemy, and she did.

The snow from the high mountain began to fall. It was an avalanche, and it was impossible for the Huns to escape it. A great wave of snow moved down and covered them all.

But the avalanche did not stop there. It continued down the mountain toward the Chinese soldiers, too.

Mulan could not run faster than an avalanche, but her horse could. She jumped on to its back and rode down the hill. Shang was still in the avalanche's path, but Mulan shouted to him, "Take my hand!"

Together they rode safely out of the avalanche's path.

After the avalanche, Shang said, "Ping, you saved my life!"

"Ping is the king of the mountains!" shouted the other soldiers. "He saved us all!"

But Mulan did not say anything. There was a terrible pain in her stomach.

"Ping, what's wrong?" Shang asked.

Mulan moved her hand from her stomach. Her fingers were red. She knew why. When she shot the cannon, Shan-Yu hit her with his sword. She fell to her knees in the snow.

"Quick!" shouted Shang. "Get help!"

Those were the last words that Mulan heard before her eyes closed.

Shang and the other soldiers waited nervously outside the little tent. Was their friend going to be okay?

At last the doctor came out. He spoke quietly to Shang. Shang's eyes opened in surprise and he ran into the tent.

Inside, Mulan was on a bed and there was a blanket around her. It was true – she was a girl!

"I ... can explain," she began.

But Chi Fu was at the entrance of the tent, too. He was very angry when he saw Mulan. He pulled her out of the tent.

"A woman!" he cried.

Chi Fu threw her down and shouted, "Snake!"

"My name is Mulan," she cried. "I did this for my father!"

Chi Fu refused to listen. He pushed a sword into Shang's hand. "You must save the honor of the Emperor's army," he said. "You must kill her!"

Shang walked toward Mulan with the sword in his hand. He looked at her for a long time. Then he threw the sword into the snow in front of her.

"A life for a life," he said.

Then he turned and left. His men followed him.

Mulan was left alone in the snow.

"Maybe I *wasn't* only trying to help my father when I joined the army," Mulan said to Mushu. "Maybe I did it for myself, too. I wanted to look in the mirror and feel proud."

Suddenly, there was a sound from a lower part of the mountain — someone was shouting angrily. Quickly, Mulan hid behind a rock and looked.

Shan-Yu was still alive! A few of his men were climbing out of the snow, too.

The Huns stood on the mountain and looked down at the Emperor's city far below them.

Mulan understood. Shan-Yu still wanted to attack the Emperor!

Mulan rode to the Emperor's city. When she arrived, the streets were full of people. They were all shouting for Shang and his men. Later there was going to be a fireworks show. But the soldiers did not seem happy. In their opinion, they did not win against the Huns in the mountains — "Ping" did.

Suddenly, Mulan was next to them. "Shang!" she cried. "The Huns are still alive. They're in the city!"

But Shang did not listen. "Go home, Mulan," he said.

"You listened to *Ping*," said Mulan. "Why is *Mulan* different?"

Shang just rode away without a word.

Mulan ran toward the palace. She tried to tell people about the Huns, but no one listened.

"It's because you are a girl," explained Mushu.

In front of the palace, the Emperor was speaking to Shang now.

"China can sleep safely because Shan-Yu is dead," he said.

But the Emperor was wrong. Suddenly Shan-Yu's men jumped out of the paper dragon behind Shang.

With swords in their hands, the Huns pushed Shang to the floor. They pulled the Emperor inside the palace and closed the palace doors behind them.

Inside Shan-Yu waited for his men to bring the Emperor to him.

Shang and his men tried to open the palace doors with a big stone dragon, but it was impossible. The doors were too big and strong.

Behind them someone shouted, "I have an idea!"

It was Mulan. Without a word, her old friends followed her.

"Put these clothes on," she cried. She threw some women's clothes to them.

Now they were not soldiers in the Chinese army. They were women of the Emperor's palace!

"We have to climb to the top of the palace," said Mulan. "Follow me!"

They used their belts to climb up the palace's big stone columns.

Outside the Emperor's room at the top of the palace, two Huns were guarding the doors. Suddenly, three women walked around the corner.

"Palace women," said one of the Huns with a big smile. He waved to the three ladies.

"*Ugly* palace women," said the other Hun.

The palace women were really Yao, Chien-Po, and Ling! When they were close enough, they pulled out their swords and started to fight the Huns. Mulan joined her friends and fought, too.

"Shang, get the Emperor!" she cried. Shang ran past the guards toward the doors to the Emperor's room.

Inside, the Emperor was standing before Shan-Yu.

"Your walls and armies have fallen," the Hun said. "Now *you* must fall to your knees, old man!"

The Emperor did not move.

Suddenly, the doors opened and Shang was there with his sword. He and Shan-Yu began to fight.

Mulan and the others ran into the room.

"Get the Emperor!" cried Mulan. Outside the window there was a long rope down to the ground.

"Use this scarf on the rope!" Mulan told Chien-Po. "Take the Emperor down safely!"

The other soldiers followed Chien-Po.

Shang and Shan-Yu were still fighting. Shang fought bravely, but the Hun was stronger than any man alive.

He stood over Shang. "I'll kill you!" he shouted angrily. "You took the Emperor away from me!"

"No, he didn't," shouted a young woman from the other side of the room. "*I* did."

At first Shan-Yu did not understand. What was this woman talking about? But then she pulled back her hair and he realized.

"You're the soldier from the mountains!" shouted Shan-Yu angrily. He dropped Shang and ran after Mulan.

She climbed out of the window and on to the palace roof.

Shan-Yu followed her. "You have no more ideas," he said.

"Not true," answered Mulan, then she shouted, "NOW, Mushu!"

Mushu shot the biggest rocket of all the palace fireworks at Shan-Yu. It hit the Hun in the chest and carried him toward a tall building with all of the other fireworks.

# BOOM!

The fireworks exploded across the sky in a thousand colors. It was the end of Shan-Yu!

Mulan ran and jumped off the roof. She caught the rope and rode it safely down to the ground.

The Emperor ordered his men to bring Mulan to him.

"I have heard about you, Mulan," he said. "You stole your father's armor and ran away from home." The Emperor smiled. "And ... you have saved us all."

He put his head down in honor of the woman who saved China. Chi Fu, Shang, and Mulan's old army friends fell to their knees in honor of her. The crowd in front of the palace did the same.

"Stay and work here at the palace," the Emperor said.

"Thank you," said Mulan. "But I would like to go home."

When Mulan arrived home, her father was in the garden.

Mulan was nervous. It was hard to find the right words.

"Father, I have brought you the sword of Shan-Yu," she said. She fell to her knees and held the sword out to her father. "It is a gift from the Emperor, to bring honor to our family."

Gifts and honor were not important to Fa Zhou any longer. There was only one important thing. His daughter was safely home at last. He took Mulan in his arms.

"You are the greatest gift of all," he told her.

Mushu was happy to be home, too. Now the family ancestors in the temple could not laugh at him.

He and the First Ancestor looked out of the temple window.

"Look!" cried Mushu. "Shang is here!"

It was true! Shang was walking into the garden.

"You ... forgot your armor," he said nervously to Mulan.

He was not really here to bring her armor. The real reason was clear. He could not forget Mulan. She was brave and smart and kind. To Shang, she was *perfect*.

Mulan smiled happily. "Would you like to stay for dinner?" she asked.

# Activity page ❶

## Before You Read

**1** **Look at the two pictures. Choose three adjectives to go with each picture.**

ⓐ _____ _____ _____     ⓑ _____ _____ _____

**2** **Answer the questions. You can use a dictionary.**
  a  Which is bigger, a **soldier** or an **army**?
  b  Which can you shoot, a **sword** or a **cannon**?
  c  Which is a person in the army, a **soldier** or an **emperor**?
  d  Which is a place for soldiers, a **camp** or a **hotel**?
  e  Which can you wear, **armor** or an **arrow**?

## After You Read

**1** **Put the sentences in the right order.**
  a  Shang discovers Mulan's secret. ☐
  b  Mushu joins Mulan near the army camp. ☐
  c  Fa Zhou learns that he must join the army. ☐ 1
  d  Mulan saves the Emperor at the palace. ☐
  e  Mulan learns that Shan-Yu did not die in the avalanche. ☐
  f  Mulan steals her father's sword and armor. ☐
  g  Fa Zhou is happy when his daughter returns home. ☐
  h  Shang teaches the new soldiers how to fight. ☐
  i  The soldiers learn that the Huns have killed everyone in the main army. ☐

# Activity page ②

**2** **Answer the questions.**
   **a** Why does Mulan join the army?
   **b** Why do her parents worry about Mulan?
   **c** Why does Mushu follow her?
   **d** Why does Chi Fu want Shang to kill Mulan in the mountains?
   **e** Why does Shang refuse to kill her?
   **f** Why does the Emperor thank Mulan?
   **g** Why does Shang come to the Fa house?

**3** **What adjective best describes Mulan? In your exercise book draw a picture of Mulan to show this. Write about your picture. What is Mulan doing? Where is she?**